I ♥ MY

||||||||||||||||||||||||||||||||||||||||||||||||||||||||||||||||||||||||||||||||||||

ICE CREAM MAKER

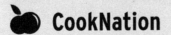 CookNation

I LOVE MY ICE CREAM MAKER
THE ONLY ICE CREAM MAKER RECIPE BOOK YOU'LL EVER NEED

ISBN 978-1-912155-11-8

DISCLAIMER

CONTENTS

SORBET 51

INTRODUCTION

Ice cream is the king of treats!

ICE CREAM

Ice Cream can be the most delightful, exciting, fun and rewarding treat for anyone, young or old. It evokes and stimulates our memories of long hot summer days and makes our taste buds scream for more. From soft and creamy classics, indulgent and rich ripples to daring, exotic and delectable concoctions, ice cream is the king of treats.

With domestic ice cream makers now established as reliable and affordable, making your own ice cream at home couldn't be easier. Recreating your favourite iced treat is simple and quick and will rival any shop-bought equivalent....you'll never want to buy a store tub of ice cream again!

Making ice cream at home can occasionally be more expensive than buying from a supermarket but the rewards in taste and texture far outweigh the difference in cost, plus your ice cream will be free from the additional preservatives and emulsifiers that commercial ice creams contain to prolong their shelf life. You can experiment with flavours and textures and make quantities to suit you and your family.

FROZEN YOGURT

Frozen yogurts, iced yogurts or 'fro-yo's' as they are also known have become a multi million dollar industry in their own right in recent years. Frozen yogurts should be consumed ideally same day but can be kept in the freezer for a few days. If you do store in the freezer, allow the yogurt to soften up in a refrigerator for 30-40 minutes before serving.

SORBET

A sorbet is a light frozen dessert, which usually contains no dairy such as cream, yogurt, milk, custard or eggs. Excellent sorbets can be made with an ice cream maker. Consistency should be slightly slushy. If you are freezing your sorbets, allow them to soften in a refrigerator for about 30 minutes before serving.

ABOUT ICE CREAM MAKERS

Domestic ice cream makers are now commonplace. There are many different models on the market ranging in price from £15 ($25) to £250 ($420) with professional models starting at £2000 ($3365)! As with all investments, your budget will dictate which type of ice cream maker you choose. There are some very good budget ice cream makers available which will make excellent ice cream, so spending more money doesn't always mean better results. However as with all electrical/mechanical appliances, the more expensive machines tend to use higher quality components, which over time may last longer than a cheaper model. You should select your model carefully based on price, customer reviews, capacity, ease of use and manufacturers guarantees & customer service.

To follow is a general guide to the 2 main types of ice cream maker currently on the market and how they work. You should of course study the manufacturers guidelines and instructions for your own model before use.

BUILT-IN FREEZER ICE CREAM MAKER

These machines have a built in freezer so there is no need to pre-freeze a bowl in the freezer before making your ice cream. It works by churning and freezing simultaneously, making ice cream from scratch in as little as 20 minutes. It will also keep your ice cream cool for up to 10 mins once churning has completed.

The machine when switched on will rapidly bring the bowl to the required temperature for making ice cream then all you need to do is switch on the paddle and add your ingredients.

Ice cream makers with a built in freezer can offer a larger capacity, but not always, so do your research before purchasing. The major advantage of this type of appliance is its ability to make different batches of ice cream one after the other. The built in freezing feature means all you need to do is clean the inner bowl then wait a few minutes for it to refreeze before starting again. No pre-planning needed. Excellent texture can also be achieved with this type of machine. If counter space is an issue you should be aware that built in freezer models tend to be larger in size and heavier than those that have a removable bowl for freezing. Built in freezing also makes this appliance more expensive.

PRE-FREEZE ICE CREAM MAKER

These are perhaps the most popular ice cream maker as they are more affordable. Unlike the built-in freezer models they require the churning bowl to be pre-frozen for a minimum of 8-12 hours in a freezer before use and therefore the cost is dramatically lower. This requires pre-planning before you can make your ice cream although you can purchase additional bowls so one can always be kept in the freezer ready to use.

The electric paddle is housed in the lid of the model and attaches to the churning bowl. Generally, smaller quantities of ice cream can be made using this type of machine and some models are less successful at preventing large ice particles forming which in turn can affect texture. Researching your model and reading customer reviews should satisfy you to this extent.

Price is the major advantage with this model although pre-freezing the bowl doesn't suit everyone.

Budget will no doubt dictate which model you choose but excellent results can be achieved in both types of machines.

TIPS

- All the recipes in this collection are simple, easy and produce great results. The quantities, timings & methods stated however may not be suitable for your individual ice cream maker so ensure you read your manufacturers instructions and follow their guidelines.

- Pre-freeze your bowl according to the manufacturers instructions. Most will advise 24 hours but some can be as little as 8 hours. Don't be tempted to freeze for less as this will affect the quality of your ice cream. Best practice is to always keep your bowl in the freezer ready to use.

- Wrap your bowl in a plastic bag before freezing. This will prevent freezer burn and ice crystals building up.

- Keep ingredients refrigerated prior to use where applicable.

- Use the freshest ingredients available and those in 'season' for the best flavour.

- Additional ingredients such as nuts, dried fruit and chocolate chips should only be added at the last minute to evenly distribute them.

- To prevent ice crystals forming on the top of ice cream, place a layer of cling film or grease proof paper over the top before putting on the lid.

- Don't store your ice cream for too long. It will lose some of its flavour and texture over time and the lack of preservatives present in shop-bought ice cream means it's best to eat as quickly as possible – ideally within a week or two weeks maximum.

- Do not refreeze ice cream that has thawed as this will pose a risk of bacteria growing.

- Thoroughly clean your ice cream maker after each batch using boiling water to sterilize.

- Do not overfill the bowl of your ice cream maker. Three quarters full should be the maximum to allow air to get into the mixture.

- After churning is complete, transfer your ice cream to the freezer for a few hours to firm up.

- To serve ice cream that has been frozen, remove from the freezer 10 minutes before serving or to the refrigerator for 30 minutes.

- To scoop ice cream perfectly from the container use a spring-loaded scoop or strong metal dessert spoon dipped in warm water.

ABOUT COOKNATION

CookNation is the leading publisher of innovative and practical recipe books for the modern cook.

With a range of #1 best-selling titles - from the innovative 'Skinny' calorie-counted series, to the 5:2 Diet Recipes collection and I Love My range - CookNation recipe books have something for everyone.

Visit **www.bellmackenzie.com** to browse the full catalogue.

 CookNation

ICE CREAM

PEACH AND RASPBERRY RIPPLE ICE CREAM

INGREDIENTS

- 300g/11oz raspberries
- 8 tbsp icing sugar
- 6 ripe peaches, peeled and stoned
- 400ml/14floz double cream

METHOD

1 First, blend the raspberries with 6 tablespoons of the icing sugar to make a puree. Sieve the mixture to remove any seeds and set to one aside.

2 Blend the peaches with the rest of the icing sugar. Gently stir in the cream. Cover and chill for 20-30 minutes.

3 Pour the peach mixture into your ice cream maker. Churn and freeze according to your device's instructions.

4 During the last 5-10 minutes churning, pour on the raspberry puree to make the ripple.

5 Serve and enjoy!

CHEFS NOTE

No need to sieve the peach puree - it will be smooth enough as it is.

BRANDY AND VANILLA ICE CREAM

INGREDIENTS

- 750ml/1¼pt double cream
- 125g/4oz caster sugar
- 1 tsp vanilla extract
- 1 vanilla pod, seeds scraped out
- 60ml/2floz brandy

METHOD

1 In a small saucepan, heat the cream, sugar, vanilla extract, and vanilla seeds until the sugar is completely dissolved.

2 Sieve into a bowl, cover, and chill for 30 minutes.

3 Stir in the brandy and pour the mixture into your ice cream maker. Churn and freeze according to your device instructions.

4 Serve and enjoy immediately

CHEFS NOTE

Use your favourite best quality brandy for top results.

CHOCOLATE ICE CREAM

INGREDIENTS

- 250g/9oz dark chocolate, broken into squares or chunks
- 100g/3½oz butter
- 150g/5oz caster sugar
- 150ml/5floz water
- 4 egg yolks
- 500ml/17floz double cream

METHOD

1 In a saucepan gently heat the chocolate and butter, stirring occasionally, until the mixture is melted and smooth. Remove from the heat.

2 Stir the sugar and water together in a clean pan over a low heat, until the sugar is dissolved. Turn up the heat and boil for a few minutes to make a syrup. Allow to cool.

3 In a bowl, whisk the egg yolks while gradually adding the cooled syrup. When the mixture is thick, whisk in the cream, then gently stir in the chocolate until well combined.

4 Cool, cover and chill in the fridge for 30 minutes.

5 Pour the mixture into your ice cream maker. Churn and freeze according to your machine's instructions.

6 Serve and enjoy!

CHEFS NOTE

For a firmer consistency, place the ice cream in the freezer for half an hour before serving.

STRAWBERRY VANILLA ICE CREAM

INGREDIENTS

- 500g/1lb 2oz strawberries, chopped
- 250ml/8½floz cream
- 250ml/8½floz milk
- 1 vanilla pod, seeds scraped out
- 100g/3½oz sugar
- 7 egg yolks
- 1 pinch salt

METHOD

1 In a pan, combine the strawberries, cream, milk, vanilla seeds and a quarter of the sugar. Bring to the boil and remove from the heat and allow to cool.

2 In a large bowl whisk together the egg yolks and the remaining sugar until smooth. Gradually whisk in the strawberries and a pinch of salt to make a custard mix.

3 Pour the custard back into the pan and warm gently until it's thick enough to coat the back of your spoon. Remove from the heat and chill thoroughly for at least 30 minutes.

4 Pour into your ice cream maker. Churn and freeze according to the device's instructions. Serve immediately, or store in the freezer.

CHEFS NOTE

Also works well with raspberries!

SUNFLOWER AND HONEY ICE CREAM

INGREDIENTS

- 250g/9oz sugar
- 3 tbsp plain flour
- ¼ tsp salt
- 2 eggs, beaten
- 600ml/1pt milk
- 500ml/17floz double cream
- 1 tbsp vanilla extract
- 60ml/2floz honey
- 1 tbsp sunflower seeds, chopped

METHOD

1 In a large bowl, whisk together all the ingredients, except the chopped sunflower seeds.

2 Cover and chill for 20 minutes.

3 Pour the mixture into your ice cream maker along with the chopped sunflower seeds. Churn and freeze according to your device's instructions.

4 Serve and enjoy!

CHEFS NOTE

If you like your ice cream harder, freeze it for up to 4 hours before serving.

GOOSEBERRY ICE CREAM

INGREDIENTS

- 500g/1lb2oz gooseberries, topped and tailed
- 3 tbsp caster sugar
- 4 tbsp water
- 4 egg yolks
- 100g/3½oz caster sugar
- 1 tsp vanilla extract
- 400ml/14floz double cream
- 200ml/7floz milk

CHEFS NOTE

Fresh gooseberries are available in season between May and September.

METHOD

1 Heat the gooseberries and sugar in a pan with 4 tbsp water. Stir gently, bring to a simmer and cook until the gooseberries start to break up and lose their shape.

2 Once this happens tip into a food processor and blend until puréed.

3 Sieve to remove the seeds and skins and put to one side to cool.

4 Meanwhile, in a large bowl, whisk the eggs, sugar and vanilla. Gently heat the milk and cream in a pan, until simmering, then gradually whisk the milk and cream into the egg mixture to make a custard.

5 Gently heat the custard, stirring continuously, until it thickens.

6 Cover and chill thoroughly in the fridge for 30 minutes.

7 Mix the gooseberry purée into the custard then pour the combined mixture into your ice-cream maker. Churn and freeze according to your machine's instructions.

8 Serve immediately or transfer to a freezer container and freeze until required.

STRAWBERRY AND MERINGUE ICE CREAM

INGREDIENTS

- 360ml/12½floz double cream
- 400ml/14floz milk
- 1 tsp vanilla essence
- 4 egg yolks
- 125g/4oz sugar
- 400g/14oz strawberries
- 2 tbsp icing sugar
- 50g/2oz meringue, crushed into small bite-sized pieces

CHEFS NOTE

Ready-made meringue nests are a handy ingredient to have for this ice cream recipe.

METHOD

1 In a bowl, whisk together the egg yolks and sugar until creamy.

2 In a saucepan, gently heat the milk and cream until the liquid begins to boil. Remove from the heat and gradually whisk into the egg mixture along with the vanilla.

3 Return the mixture to the pan on a low heat, stirring continuously until it thickens. Remove from the heat and cool, cover and refrigerate for 30 minutes.

4 Blend the strawberries and icing sugar until smooth. Sieve to remove any pips. Heat the strawberry purée in a small pan and bring to the boil. Simmer until the purée thickens like jam. Cool and refrigerate.

5 Pour the vanilla cream mixture into your ice cream maker. Churn and freeze according to your device's instructions. Around five minutes before the ice cream is ready, open the lid and sprinkle in the meringue pieces.

6 When these are churned in, drizzle in the strawberry puree for just a few seconds to give a ripple effect.

7 Serve immediately or freeze in a freezer container.

LEMON CURD ICE CREAM

INGREDIENTS

- 300ml/10½floz condensed milk
- 2 tbsp skimmed milk powder
- 2 tsp vanilla extract
- 500ml/17floz semi-skimmed milk
- 120ml/4floz double cream
- 250g/9oz lemon curd, chilled

METHOD

1 In a bowl, whisk the condensed milk with the milk powder and vanilla. Whisk in the semi-skimmed milk and cream until smooth.

2 Cover and chill for 20 minutes.

3 Pour this into your ice cream maker along with the lemon curd. Churn and freeze according to the device's instructions.

4 Serve immediately, or transfer to a freezer container and freeze for around 4 hours for a firmer consistency.

CHEFS NOTE

Pre-made lemon curd is the easiest cheat ingredient for this ice cream but you can make your own too if you prefer.

MELON ICE CREAM

INGREDIENTS

- 300ml/10½floz double cream
- 175g/6oz caster sugar
- 1 Cantaloupe melon, peeled, deseeded & chopped
- 1 tbsp lemon juice

METHOD

1 In a pan, bring the cream and sugar to the boil, stirring to dissolve the sugar. Remove from the heat and set aside.

2 Use a blender to blend the melon with the lemon juice until smooth. Pour the cream mixture in and blend again.

3 Cover and chill for 30 minutes, then pour into your ice-cream maker. Churn and freeze according to your device's instructions.

4 Serve immediately, or transfer to a freezer container and freeze for a firmer consistency.

CHEFS NOTE

For the best tasting results make sure your melon is very ripe.

COFFEE ICE CREAM

INGREDIENTS

- 8 egg yolks
- 175g/6oz sugar
- 400ml/14floz double cream
- 400ml/14floz milk
- 120ml/4floz espresso coffee

METHOD

1 In a bowl, whisk the egg yolks and sugar until smooth.

2 In a pan, bring the cream, milk and coffee to the boil then remove from the heat. Gradually whisk it into the egg mixture until well combined.

3 Pour the mixture into a pan and heat slowly to thicken.

4 Sieve the mixture into a bowl to cool, then cover and chill in the fridge for 30 minutes.

5 Once cold, pour the mixture into your ice cream maker. Churn and freeze according to your device's instructions.

6 Enjoy immediately, or store in the freezer until required.

CHEFS NOTE

Adjust the quantity of coffee to suit your own taste.

MINT CHOCOLATE CHIP ICE CREAM

INGREDIENTS

- 750ml/1¼pts single cream
- 5 egg yolks, beaten
- 150g/5oz caster sugar
- 3 tbsp crème de menthe
- 50g/2oz milk chocolate chips

METHOD

1 In a pan, heat the cream, egg yolks and sugar, stirring frequently. Just before boiling, remove from the heat and pour into a bowl to cool.

2 When its cooled stir in the crème de menthe and chocolate. Cover and chill for 30 minutes.

3 Pour the mixture into your ice cream maker. Churn and freeze according to the machine's instructions.

4 Serve immediately and enjoy!

CHEFS NOTE

Peppermint extract will also work in place of crème de menthe.

CINNAMON ICE CREAM

INGREDIENTS

- 360ml/12½floz semi-skimmed milk
- 225g/8oz sugar
- 1 tsp vanilla extract
- 2 cinnamon sticks
- 5 large egg yolks
- 360ml/12½floz double cream
- 1 tsp ground cinnamon

METHOD

1 Heat the milk and sugar in a pan, stirring to dissolve the sugar. Add the vanilla extract and cinnamon sticks. Heat to just below boiling.

2 Meanwhile, in a bowl, whisk the egg yolks until they turn paler.

3 Remove the cinnamon sticks from the warm milk. Gradually whisk a few splashes of the milk mixture into the eggs. Then stir the eggs slowly into the pan. Cook for about 2 minutes until it begins to thicken.

4 Sieve the mixture into a bowl. Stir in the cream, then whisk in the ground cinnamon. Cover and chill thoroughly in the fridge for at least 30 minutes.

5 Pour the mixture into your ice cream maker. Churn and freeze according to your device instructions.

6 Serve immediately, or freeze for a firmer consistency.

CHEFS NOTE

Delicious served with cinnamon swirls.

COCONUT LIME & BLUEBERRY ICE CREAM

INGREDIENTS

- 2 tbsp lime juice
- Zest from 1 lime
- 140g/4½oz caster sugar
- 125g/4oz blueberries
- 200ml/7floz coconut cream
- 300ml/10½floz double cream

METHOD

1 In a small pan, heat the lime juice, zest and the sugar, stirring to dissolve the sugar. Add the blueberries and simmer for a few minutes, until the blueberry skins begin to split.

2 Remove from the heat and pour into a bowl. Whisk in the coconut cream and the cream, cover and chill in the fridge for 30 minutes.

3 Pour the mixture into your ice cream maker. Churn and freeze according to your machine's instructions.

4 Serve immediately, or transfer to a freezer container and freeze for a few hours to firm the consistency.

CHEFS NOTE

This zingy ice cream is delicious served with a scattering of extra fresh blueberries.

RASPBERRY ICE CREAM

INGREDIENTS

- 600g/1lb 5oz raspberries
- 175g/6oz sugar
- 200ml/7floz double cream
- 200ml/7floz semi-skimmed milk
- 4 large egg yolks
- 2 tbsp powdered milk
- 1½ tsp vanilla extract

CHEFS NOTE

Sieve the raspberry puree to remove the seeds for a smoother texture.

METHOD

1 Blend the raspberries into a puree, and set aside.

2 In a pan gently heat the sugar, cream & milk, stirring to dissolve the sugar. Keep warm over a low heat, without boiling.

3 Meanwhile, in a bowl, whisk the egg yolks until thickened. Gradually whisk in a few splashes of the hot milk mixture. Then stir the egg mixture into the saucepan to make a custard.

4 Turn up the heat and stir constantly until the custard thickens. Stir in the powdered milk and remove from the heat.

5 Sieve into a bowl and combine with the raspberry puree and vanilla extract. Allow to cool, cover and chill in the fridge for 30 minutes.

6 When thoroughly cold, pour into your ice cream maker. Churn and freeze according to your machine's instructions. Serve immediately, or freeze until required.

SPICED MAPLE ICE CREAM

INGREDIENTS

- ½ tsp vanilla extract
- 360ml/12½floz milk
- 360ml/12½floz double cream
- 10 allspice berries
- 6 cloves
- 4 cinnamon sticks
- Pinch ground nutmeg
- 100g/3½oz brown sugar
- 250ml/8½floz pure maple syrup
- 7 egg yolks
- Pinch salt
- 1 tsp maple essence

CHEFS NOTE

Try served with chopped candied maple nuts over the top.

METHOD

1 In a saucepan gently heat the milk, cream, spices and sugar. Stir to dissolve the sugar. Remove from heat, cover and leave for an hour.

2 Meanwhile, simmer the maple syrup in another pan over a medium heat until it reduces by about a third of its volume.

3 Whisk the egg yolks and salt in a large bowl.

4 Return the cream mixture to a simmer and stir in the maple syrup.

5 Whisking the eggs, gradually add some of the hot maple cream mixture. Pour the combined mixture back into the pan and cook over medium heat without boiling, stirring constantly, until the custard thickens.

6 Sieve the custard into a bowl and stir in the vanilla & maple essences. Allow to cool, cover and chill for 30 minutes in the fridge.

7 When the mixture is chilled pour it into your ice cream maker. Churn and freeze according to the device instructions.

8 Serve at once, or freeze until required.

LIQUORICE ICE CREAM

INGREDIENTS

- 250ml/8½floz double cream
- 250ml/8½floz milk
- 100g/3½oz sugar
- 25g/1oz liquorice powder
- 6 egg yolks

METHOD

1 In a large pan heat the cream, milk, sugar and liquorice up to boiling point. Remove from the heat.

2 In a bowl, beat the eggs. Once the liquorice cream mixture boils, pour some of it very gradually over the yolks, stirring constantly so that the eggs don't scramble.

3 When well combined, cover the bowl and leave to cool to room temperature. Then chill in the fridge for 30 minutes.

4 Pour the mixture into your ice cream maker. Churn and freeze according to your machine's instructions.

5 Serve and enjoy!

CHEFS NOTE

Liquorice powder is made from liquorice root and is available from specialist or health shops.

COCONUT AVOCADO ICE CREAM

INGREDIENTS

- 2 x 400ml/14floz cans coconut milk
- 2 medium avocados, peeled and stoned
- 1 medium banana, peeled
- Zest of 1 lime
- 1 tbsp lime juice
- 1 tsp vanilla essence
- 3 tbsp agave nectar

METHOD

1 In a small pan, gently heat the coconut milk, agave nectar, lime juice & zest until combined and smooth.

2 Leave to cool then blend with the rest of the ingredients until smooth.

3 Cover and chill for 30 minutes. Pour the mixture into your ice cream maker. Churn and freeze according to your device's instructions.

4 Serve immediately, or freeze until required.

CHEFS NOTE

A super smooth refreshing ice cream!

BLACKBERRY CHOC CHIP ICE CREAM

INGREDIENTS

- 450g/1lb blackberries
- 275g/10oz sugar
- 1 tbsp lemon juice
- 360ml/12½floz single cream
- 5 egg yolks
- 360ml/12½floz double cream
- 125g/4oz milk chocolate chips

CHEFS NOTE

If you prefer, use dark chocolate chips instead of milk.

METHOD

1 In a pan, gently heat the blackberries, 1 tbsp of the sugar and the lemon juice, until the fruit begins to stew and becomes syrupy.

2 Sieve the mixture into a bowl, squeezing out as much of the liquid as you possibly can. Set aside to cool.

3 In another pan, heat the single cream and the remaining sugar over a medium heat and stir until the sugar is dissolved.

4 In a bowl, whisk the egg yolks until they thicken. Spoon a little of the warm cream into the yolks, whisking constantly. Then pour the eggs into the saucepan, stirring gently to make a custard.

5 When it thickens a little remove from the heat combine into the bowl with the berries. Add the double cream and mix well. Cover and chill for 30 minutes.

6 Pour the mixture into your ice cream maker. Churn and freeze according to your device's instructions. In the last couple of minutes, add the chocolate chunks to the ice cream.

7 Serve and enjoy!

GINGER ICE CREAM

INGREDIENTS

- 600ml/1pt milk
- 225g/8oz clotted cream
- 1 tsp vanilla extract
- 6 egg yolks
- 75g/3oz caster sugar
- 100g/3½oz stem ginger from a jar, finely chopped, plus 6 tbsp of the syrup
- from the jar

METHOD

1 In a pan, heat the milk and clotted cream until almost boiling then set to one side.

2 In a bowl, whisk together the egg and sugar and carefully pour the milk mixture over the eggs, stirring constantly.

3 Wash the pan and sieve the mixture into it. Heat gently without boiling, stirring constantly, until the mixture thickens a little. Pour back into the bowl and leave to cool.

4 Cover the bowl and chill for at least 30 minutes, until thoroughly cold.

5 Stir the stem ginger and syrup into the mixture, then pour it into your ice-cream maker. Churn and freeze, according to your device's instructions.

6 Serve immediately, or freeze until required.

CHEFS NOTE

Use double cream instead of clotted cream if you prefer.

PLUM RIPPLE ICE CREAM

INGREDIENTS

- 250ml/8½floz milk
- 250ml/8½floz double cream
- 1 tsp vanilla essence
- 6 egg yolks
- 325g/11oz sugar
- 300g/11oz fresh plums
- 100ml/3½floz water

CHEFS NOTE

Use ripe plums for the best taste.

METHOD

1 In a pan gently heat the milk & cream.

2 Meanwhile, whisk together the egg yolks and about a third of the sugar until they thicken. When the cream mixture comes to the boil, remove from the heat and pour gradually over the eggs, whisking continuously until fully combined.

3 Pour back into the pan and warm over a low-medium heat. Stir constantly until the mixture thickens. Remove from the heat and sieve into a bowl. Cool, cover and chill in the fridge for 30 minutes.

4 Meanwhile, place the plums in a pan with the water and the rest of the sugar. Bring to the boil, cover and simmer for 10 minutes until the plums begin to stew.

5 Remove from the heat and sieve the mixture into a bowl. Allow to cool, then chill in the fridge until needed.

6 When the cream mixture is thoroughly cold, pour it into your ice cream maker. Churn and freeze according to your machine's instructions. Add the plum purée and churn for another few minutes to make the ripple effect.

7 Serve and enjoy!

ALMOND ICE CREAM

INGREDIENTS

- 50g/2oz caster sugar
- 300ml/10½floz double cream
- 1 tbsp ground almonds
- 2 tbsp icing sugar
- 1 tsp almond extract
- 500g/1lb2oz tub ready-made vanilla custard
- 2 tbsp toasted flaked almonds

METHOD

1 In a large bowl combine the cream, icing sugar, ground almonds & almond extract. Whip the cream until thickened then fold in the custard.

2 Cover and chill in the fridge for 30 minutes.

3 Pour the custard mixture into your ice-cream maker. Churn and freeze according to your machine's instructions. Serve immediately scattered with toasted almonds.

CHEFS NOTE

This simple ice cream has a triple almond kick.

SIMPLE CHOCOLATE ICE CREAM

INGREDIENTS

- 4 egg yolks
- 75g/3oz cocoa powder
- 100g/3½oz sugar
- 2 tbsp milk
- 360ml/12½floz single cream
- 360ml/12½floz double cream
- 1 tsp vanilla extract
- 100g/3½oz dark chocolate, chopped
- 2 tsp chocolate curls

CHEFS NOTE

Use chopped milk chocolate rather than dark chocolate if you prefer.

METHOD

1 In a bowl, whisk the egg yolks with the cocoa, sugar and milk, until dark brown and thickened.

2 Heat the single and double cream in a pan over medium-low heat to simmering point but don't boil.

3 Gradually, whisk about half the cream mixture into the egg and cocoa in the bowl, until the liquids are well blended.

4 Add the chopped chocolate to the cream mixture remaining in the pan, and stir until it melts. Pour the cocoa mixture from the bowl into the pan and cook over low heat, stirring occasionally for a few minutes, until the custard thickens.

5 Remove from the heat and leave to cool to room temperature. Pour into a bowl, add the vanilla extract, cover and chill in the fridge for 30 minutes.

6 Pour the chilled custard into your ice cream maker. Churn and freeze according to the device's instructions.

7 Serve immediately, garnished with chocolate curls.

CHOCOLATE COOKIE ICE CREAM

INGREDIENTS

- 750ml/1¼pt milk
- 250ml/8½floz double cream
- 6 egg yolks
- 140g/4½oz sugar
- 100g/3½oz milk chocolate, chopped
- 140g/4½oz Ovaltine powder
- 150g/5oz packet cookies, broken into chunks

METHOD

1 In a pan bring the milk and cream to a simmer.

2 In a bowl whisk the egg yolks and sugar together.

3 Pour the milk onto the eggs, stirring constantly. Wash the pan and pour the mixture back in. Heat gently for about 10 minutes, stirring constantly until it's thickened.

4 Put the chopped chocolate into a bowl, and pour the custard over the top. When the chocolate has melted, whisk in the Ovaltine.

5 Cool, cover and chill for 30 minutes.

6 Pour the mixture into your ice-cream maker. Churn and freeze according to your device's instructions. Add the biscuit chunks and churn for a few minutes more.

CHEFS NOTE

Try serving with white chocolate sauce!

WHISKY ICE CREAM

INGREDIENTS

- 125g/4oz sugar
- 50g/2oz liquid glucose
- 8 egg yolks
- 250ml/8½floz milk
- 250ml/8½floz double cream
- 25ml/1floz whisky

METHOD

1 In a large bowl, whisk together the sugar, glucose and egg yolks.

2 In a pan combine the milk and cream. Gently heat until just below boiling.

3 Whisking constantly, gradually pour the hot cream over the eggs. Return the mixture to the pan and heat gently until it thickens.

4 Remove from the heat and stir in the whisky. Leave to cool, cover and chill for 30 minutes.

5 Pour into your ice cream maker. Churn and freeze according to your machine's instructions.

CHEFS NOTE

Use a good quality single malt whisky for the best flavour.

EGG NOG ICE CREAM

INGREDIENTS

- 4 egg yolks
- 75g/3oz sugar
- 600ml/1pt whole milk
- 250ml/8½floz double cream
- 1 tsp freshly grated nutmeg
- 100ml/3½floz bourbon

METHOD

1 In a bowl, whisk together the egg yolks and sugar until the sugar is completely dissolved.

2 In a pan combine the milk, cream & nutmeg. Bring to the boil, stirring occasionally. Remove from the heat and gradually add the hot cream to the eggs, whisking constantly.

3 Pour the egg mixture back into the pan and stirring constantly over a medium heat until it thickens.

4 Remove from the heat, stir in the bourbon and pour into a medium bowl. Leave to cool, then chill in the fridge for 30 minutes.

5 When it's thoroughly cold, pour the mixture into your ice cream maker. Churn and freeze according to the device's instructions.

6 Serve immediately or, for a firmer consistency, transfer to a freezer container and freeze for 2-4 hours.

CHEFS NOTE

Rum or brandy will work in place of bourbon.

COOKIE DOUGH ICE CREAM

INGREDIENTS

- 600ml/1pt double cream
- 1 tsp vanilla extract
- 100g/3½oz caster sugar
- 4 egg yolks
- 300g/11oz packet chocolate chip cookie dough

METHOD

1 Whisk together the sugar and egg yolks until they begin to thicken.

2 Add the cream and cook gently on a low heat until it thickens a little.

3 Pour into a bowl, leave to cool then chill in the fridge for 30 minutes.

4 Meanwhile roll out the cookie dough and dice into small cubes.

5 When the mixture is thoroughly cold stir on the vanilla extract and pour it into your ice cream maker.

6 Churn until it's thickened then add cookie dough pieces. Churn for a minute or two longer and place in the freezer to freeze until completely solid.

CHEFS NOTE

Ready made cookie dough is available in most large supermarkets.

APRICOT ICE CREAM

INGREDIENTS

- 4 egg yolks
- 150g/5oz sugar, plus 25g/1oz
- 600ml/1pt milk
- 120ml/4floz double cream
- Pinch salt
- 250g/9oz apricots, peeled, stoned and chopped
- 100ml/3½oz water

METHOD

1 In a bowl whisk together the egg yolks and sugar until the sugar has dissolved.

2 Combine the milk, cream and salt in a pan. Heat until almost boiling before removing from the heat.

3 Gradually add the hot cream to the eggs, whisking constantly.

4 Pour the egg mixture back into the pan and gently heat until it begins to thicken – stirring constantly.

5 Pour the mixture into a bowl and leave to cool, then chill in the fridge for 30 minutes.

6 Meanwhile heat the chopped apricots in a pan with the sugar and water. Cook until softened then blend to a puree.

7 Combine together the cream mixture and the apricot puree, then pour into your ice cream maker. Churn and freeze according to your device's instructions.

8 Serve and enjoy!

CHEFS NOTE

You can also use tinned apricots if that's what you have to hand.

CHUNKY PEACH ICE CREAM

INGREDIENTS

- 3 egg yolks
- 165g/5½oz light brown sugar
- 360ml/12½floz double cream
- 360ml/12½floz whole milk
- 1 tbsp fresh lemon juice
- 1 tsp vanilla essence
- 3 large peaches, peeled, stoned & chopped

METHOD

1 In a large bowl, whisk together the egg yolks and sugar.

2 Bring the cream and milk to a gentle simmer in a pan over a low heat.

3 Gradually pour the hot milk into the egg mixture, constantly whisking, until thoroughly combined.

4 Pour the whole mixture back into the saucepan. Continue stirring over a low heat until the custard has thickened.

5 Sieve the custard into a bowl. Leave to cool, then chill in the fridge for 30 minutes.

6 When the custard is thoroughly cold, stir in the lemon juice and vanilla essence. Pour it all into your ice cream maker. Churn and freeze according to the device's instructions. Add the peach chunks halfway through the churning process.

CHEFS NOTE

Substitute for tinned peaches if you prefer.

BALSAMIC STRAWBERRY ICE CREAM

INGREDIENTS

- 300ml/10½floz milk
- 300ml/10½floz double cream
- 2 tsp vanilla extract
- 3 large egg yolks
- 100g/3½oz caster sugar
- 600g/1lb 5oz strawberries, chopped
- 4 tbsp icing sugar, to taste
- 4 tbsp white balsamic vinegar
- 1 tsp lemon juice

CHEFS NOTE

To remove all the strawberries seeds sieve the puree before adding to the custard.

METHOD

1 In a pan heat the milk & cream until just boiling. Remove from the heat and stir in the vanilla extract.

2 In a bowl, whisk together the egg yolks and caster sugar.

3 Gradually, pour the warm milk over the egg, whisking constantly. Pour the combined mixture into a clean pan and cook gently, without boiling, stirring continuously, until it thickens enough to coat the back of your spoon.

4 Pour the custard into a bowl and set it aside to cool. Then chill in the fridge for 30 minutes.

5 Meanwhile, blend the strawberries with the icing sugar and balsamic vinegar into a puree.

6 When the custard is thoroughly chilled, stir in the strawberry purée. Add a little lemon juice to taste.

7 Pour the mixture into your ice cream maker. Churn and freeze according to your device's instructions.

8 Serve immediately, or for a firmer ice cream, transfer to a freezer container, and freeze for 2 hours or so.

EASY CARIBBEAN ICE CREAM

INGREDIENTS

- 4 ripe bananas
- 600g/1pt double cream
- 300g/11oz caster sugar
- 100ml/3½floz rum

METHOD

1 Use a blender to blend the bananas, cream, sugar & rum until smooth.

2 Chill in the fridge for 20 minutes.

3 Pour into your ice cream maker, churn and freeze according to the device's directions.

4 Serve immediately, or transfer to a freezer container and freeze until you need it.

CHEFS NOTE

Bananas make this super-easy ice cream nice & creamy.

PISTACHIO ICE CREAM

INGREDIENTS

- 150g/5oz pistachios, raw, shelled
- 600ml/1pt milk
- 200ml/7floz double cream
- 150g/5oz sugar
- Pinch salt
- 1 tbsp syrup
- 4 egg yolks

CHEFS NOTE

Serve this scattered with some freshly chopped pistachios.

METHOD

1 Preheat the oven to 180°C and gently toast the nuts on a baking tray for 5-10 minutes. Finely chop and put to one side.

2 In a large pan, heat the pistachios, milk, cream, salt and half the sugar. Bring the mixture to the boil, remove from the heat, cover and leave to infuse for at least 30 minutes. Strain the milk into a pan and discard the pistachios.

3 Return the milk to the pan over a medium heat and bring to the boil.

4 Meanwhile, in a bowl, whisk together the egg yolks and the remaining sugar. When the milk just reaches boiling remove from the heat and gradually add to the eggs - whisking all the time.

5 Pour the eggs into the pan and stir constantly until the custard has thickened.

6 Pour the custard into a bowl and cool to room temperature. Cover and chill in the fridge for 30 minutes.

7 Pour into your ice cream maker. Churn and freeze, following the device's instructions.

8 Serve and enjoy!

BARLEY ICE CREAM

INGREDIENTS

- 600ml/1pt whole milk
- 200g/7oz pearl barley
- 100g/3½oz caster sugar
- 6 egg yolks

METHOD

1 Preheat the oven to 180°C. Toast the barley on a baking tray for about 10 minutes until dark golden in colour.

2 Pour the barley into a pan with the milk and bring to the boil. Remove from the heat and leave to infuse for at least 2 hours.

3 Sieve the mixture into a pan. Add the sugar and bring to the boil, stirring occasionally to dissolve the sugar. Remove from the heat

4 Whisk the egg yolks in a bowl. Whisking constantly, gradually pour the milk onto the eggs until fully blended.

5 Pour the mixture back into the pan and cook on low heat, without boiling, until the custard is thickened.

6 Pour into a bowl and set it aside to cool. Then, cover and chill in the fridge for 30 minutes.

7 Pour into your ice cream maker. Churn and freeze according to your device's instructions.

8 Serve at once, or store in the freezer until required.

CHEFS NOTE

This ice cream has a subtle, nutty flavour. blurb

WHISKY AND CHOC CHIP ICE CREAM

INGREDIENTS

- 4 egg yolks
- 60ml/2floz whiskey
- 125g/4oz sugar
- 360ml/12½floz double cream
- 1 tsp vanilla extract
- 125g/4oz milk chocolate chips

METHOD

1 In a bowl, whisk together the egg yolks, whisky and half the sugar. Set aside.

2 In a pan, gently heat the cream, and the remaining sugar. Stir well, and simmer gently until the sugar is dissolved.

3 Remove the pan from the heat and gradually pour on to the egg mixture, stirring constantly. Return the combined mixture to the pan, and cook on low heat, without boiling, stirring constantly until thickened.

4 Pour into clean bowl and leave to cool. Cover and chill in the fridge for 30 minutes.

5 When thoroughly cold, stir in the chocolate chips and vanilla extract. Pour into your ice cream maker. Churn and freeze according to your machine's instructions.

6 Serve and enjoy!

CHEFS NOTE

For a more grown up ice cream use dark chocolate chips instead of milk.

FRESH MINT ICE CREAM

INGREDIENTS

- 450ml/15½floz milk
- 120ml/4floz double cream
- 125g/4oz caster sugar
- 40g/1½oz milk powder
- 50g/2oz fresh mint leaves

METHOD

1 Gently heat the milk and cream in a pan with the sugar and milk powder until just below boiling. Stir in the mint leaves, remove from the heat and blend until completely smooth.

2 Allow to cool to room temperature, cover and chill in the fridge for at least 30 minutes.

3 Churn and freeze in your ice cream maker, according to the device's instructions.

4 Serve at once, or for a firmer consistency, transfer to a freezer container and freeze for up to 4 hours.

CHEFS NOTE

You may wish to use peppermint extract in place of fresh mint.

CARAMEL COCONUT ICE CREAM

INGREDIENTS

- 2 x 400ml/14floz coconut milk
- 200g/7oz brown sugar
- ½ tsp salt
- 6 egg yolks
- 1 tsp vanilla extract

METHOD

1 In a pan, heat half of the coconut milk along with all the brown sugar and salt.

2 Bring to the boil, stirring occasionally to dissolve the sugar. Reduce the heat and continue to cook for about 25 minutes until the mixture has darkened and thickened like caramel. Stir in the rest of the coconut milk and remove from the heat.

3 Whisk the egg yolks in a large bowl and gradually add the hot caramel mixture from the pan into the yolks – whisking constantly.

4 Turn the heat right down under the pan, and pour in the egg mixture, continuing to stir constantly until everything thickens up.

5 Remove from the heat and pour into a bowl. Stir in the vanilla extract. Leave to cool, cover and chill in the fridge for 30 minutes.

6 When the mixture is thoroughly cold, pour it into your ice cream maker. Churn and freeze following your device's directions.

7 Serve at once, or for a firmer consistency, transfer to a freezer container and freeze for up to 4 hours.

CHEFS NOTE

Coconut milk is a great non-dairy alternative for ice cream making.

PECAN ICE CREAM

INGREDIENTS

- 200g/7oz light brown sugar
- 120ml/4floz water
- Pinch salt
- 2 large egg yolks
- 25g/1oz unsalted butter
- 250ml/8½floz milk
- 1 tsp vanilla extract
- 250ml/8½floz double cream
- 125g/4oz toasted pecan nuts, chopped

METHOD

1 In a pan, heat the brown sugar, water and salt. Bring to the boil, stirring to dissolve the sugar into a syrup. Allow to boil for 2 minutes.

2 Meanwhile, whisk the egg yolks in a bowl and gradually whisk in the syrup from the pan.

3 Return all the mixture to the pan and cook gently, without boiling, stirring constantly. When the mixture thickens stir in the butter until melted.

4 Sieve into a clean bowl and cool, then chill, covered, in the fridge for at least 30 minutes.

5 When thoroughly chilled, stir in the milk, cream and vanilla.

6 Pour it all into your ice cream maker. Churn and freeze according to the device's directions. Sprinkle in the chopped pecans, then churn for another few minutes, and serve.

CHEFS NOTE

Any type of nut you prefer will work for this buttery ice cream.

ROCKY ROAD ICE CREAM

INGREDIENTS

- 500ml/17floz double cream
- 3 tbsp cocoa powder
- 150g/5oz milk chocolate, finely chopped
- 250ml/8½floz milk
- 175g/6oz sugar
- Pinch salt
- 5 egg yolks
- ½ tsp vanilla extract
- 50g/2oz miniature marshmallows, chopped
- 125g/4oz walnuts, chopped
- 75g/3oz glacé cherries, chopped

CHEFS NOTE

Use whichever nuts you prefer for this classic rocky road recipe.

METHOD

1 In a pan, whisk together half the cream and the cocoa powder, and bring to the boil. Lower the heat and simmer for about a minute, whisking constantly.

2 Remove from the heat and stir in the chopped chocolate until smooth. Add the remaining cream. Pour the mixture into a large bowl and set aside.

3 In another pan, heat the milk, sugar, and salt to just below boiling.

4 In a bowl whisk the egg yolks, then gradually pour the warm milk from the pan into the egg yolks, whisking constantly until blended. Pour the combined mixture back into the pan.

5 Stirring constantly, cook gently until the mixture thickens. Remove from the heat then stir in the vanilla extract.

6 Cool the custard, cover and chill in the fridge for 30 minutes.

7 Pour into your ice cream maker. Churn and freeze according to your machine's instructions. Add the marshmallows, walnuts & cherries for the last minute or two of churning.

8 Serve immediately.

EASY 'CHEATS' VANILLA ICE CREAM

INGREDIENTS

- 1 tsp vanilla extract
- 500g/1lb2oz vanilla custard
- 300ml/10½floz double cream

METHOD

1 Mix all the ingredients together in a bowl.

2 Cover and chill for 20 minutes in the fridge, then pour into your ice cream maker. Churn and freeze according to your device instructions.

3 Serve immediately, on its own or as an accompaniment to fresh fruit.

CHEFS NOTE

Make sure you use good quality custard to get the best from this simple recipe.

♥

SORBET

CHOCOLATE MINT SORBET

INGREDIENTS

- 1lt/1½pt water
- 175g/6oz sugar
- 60ml/2floz light corn syrup
- 1 tbsp cocoa powder
- 125g/4oz dark chocolate, chopped
- 4 drops peppermint oil

METHOD

1 In pan, heat the water, sugar and syrup and bring to the boil and stir until the sugar dissolves.

2 Mix the cocoa and chocolate in a bowl. Pour the hot syrup mixture over the top. Leave for 2 minutes, then whisk together until smooth. Stir in the peppermint extract. Allow to cool, cover and chill for 30 minutes in the fridge.

3 Pour the mixture into your ice-cream maker. Churn and freeze following the device instructions.

4 Serve immediately or transfer to a container and store in the freezer until needed.

CHEFS NOTE

For a delicious and simple chocolate sorbet, simply omit the peppermint oil.

LIMONCELLO SORBET

INGREDIENTS

- 375g/13oz caster sugar
- 450ml/15½floz water
- Juice and zest of 2 lemons
- 120ml/4floz limoncello
- 1 tsp lemon extract

METHOD

1 In a pan, gently heat the sugar and water until the sugar dissolves. Boil for a couple of minutes until the mixture becomes syrupy.

2 Pour the syrup into a bowl and add all the other ingredients. Cool, cover and chill in the fridge for 30 minutes.

3 Pour into your ice cream maker to churn and freeze according to your device's instructions.

CHEFS NOTE

Limoncello is a refreshing and delicious liqueur made in Italy but widely available in the UK.

STRAWBERRY SORBET

INGREDIENTS

- 450g/1lb strawberries, husks removed
- 600ml/1pt water
- 450g/1lb caster sugar

METHOD

1 In a pan heat the water and sugar. Bring to the boil until the sugar dissolves completely and the liquid grows syrupy. Set aside to cool.

2 Blend the strawberries with a little of the syrup to make a puree. Sieve the puree into a bowl and then stir in the rest of the syrup.

3 Cover and chill in the fridge for 30 minutes.

4 Pour into your ice cream maker. Churn and freeze according to your device's directions.

5 Eat immediately, or transfer to a freezer container and freeze for later.

CHEFS NOTE

Delicious also with raspberries instead of strawberries.

LEMON AND STRAWBERRY SORBET

INGREDIENTS

- 2-3 tbsp lemon juice
- 400g/14oz caster sugar
- 900g/2lb strawberries, chopped

METHOD

1 Mix the lemon juice and sugar together.

2 Blend the strawberries to a puree and stir this into the lemon sugar.

3 Cover and chill for 20 minutes.

4 Pour the mixture into your ice-cream maker. Churn and freeze according to your device's instructions.

5 Serve and enjoy!

CHEFS NOTE

Sieve the blended strawberries if you wish to remove the seeds.

CRANBERRY AND RASPBERRY SORBET

INGREDIENTS

- 350g/12oz caster sugar
- 450ml/15½floz water
- 200g/7oz frozen cranberries
- 350g/12oz frozen raspberries
- 360ml/12½floz cherry juice
- 2 tbsp lime juice
- 2 tbsp orange juice

METHOD

1 In a pan, heat the sugar and water until the sugar is all dissolved. Stir in the cranberries and cook, stirring for 5 minutes. Add the raspberries and cook 5 minutes or until the raspberries have softened and the cranberries have burst.

2 Sieve the mixture into a bowl, and cool. Chill in the fridge for 30 minutes, stir in the cherry juice, lime juice and orange juice.

3 Pour the mixture into your ice cream maker. Churn and freeze, following your device's directions.

4 Serve at once, or transfer to a container and freeze for 2 hours for a firmer consistency.

CHEFS NOTE

Using frozen fruit makes this recipe quick and easy, but you can also use fresh berries.

MIXED BERRY SORBET

INGREDIENTS

- 500g/1lb2oz mixed berries
- 250g/9oz caster sugar
- 1 tbsp lemon juice
- Splash of water

METHOD

1 Add all the ingredients to a pan and bring to simmer until the sugar dissolves. Remove from the heat and cool.

2 Blend the mixture, then sieve to make a smooth purée. Cover and chill in the fridge for 30 minutes.

3 Pour into your ice cream maker. Freeze and churn according to the device instructions.

4 Eat at once, or, for a firmer sorbet, freeze the mixture for a further 30 minutes or so.

CHEFS NOTE

Frozen mixed berries work just as well for this recipe.

COFFEE AND CHOCOLATE SORBET

INGREDIENTS

- 225g/8oz sugar
- 50g/2oz cocoa powder
- ¼ tsp vanilla extract
- Pinch ground cinnamon
- Pinch salt
- 500ml/17floz water
- 25ml/1floz espresso
- 1½ tbsp coffee liqueur

METHOD

1 Combine all the ingredients except coffee liqueur in large pan. Heat gently until everything is blended and dissolved. Remove from the heat and stir in the coffee liqueur.

2 Pour the mixture into a bowl to cool. Cover and chill in the fridge for 30 minutes.

3 When the mixture is thoroughly cold, pour into your ice cream maker. Churn and freeze, following your device instructions.

4 If the sorbet is still too soft to scoop, transfer it to a container and freeze for an hour before serving.

CHEFS NOTE

Get the best chocolate flavour by using a high quality cocoa.

TANGERINE SORBET

INGREDIENTS

- 125g/4oz sugar
- 175ml/6floz water
- 8 tangerines, peeled and quartered
- 1 tbsp lemon juice
- 1 egg white

METHOD

1 Gently heat the sugar and water in a pan, stirring until the sugar has dissolved. Bring to the boil for about 3 minutes until the liquid becomes syrupy. Set aside to cool.

2 Meanwhile, blend the tangerines to a puree. Sieve the puree into a bowl. Mix in the sugar syrup and the lemon juice. Cover and chill for 30 minutes.

3 Fold in the egg white. Pour the mixture into your ice cream maker. Churn and freeze according to your device's instructions.

4 Eat at once or transfer to a freezer container and freeze until required.

CHEFS NOTE

Substitute 3 oranges for the tangerines if you wish.

DOUBLE RASPBERRY SORBET

INGREDIENTS

- 125g/4oz caster sugar
- 150ml/5floz water
- 1 tbsp lemon juice
- 300g/11oz raspberries
- 1 tsp natural raspberry flavouring

METHOD

1 In a pan, gently heat the sugar and water until the sugar dissolves. Boil for a couple of minutes until the liquid becomes syrupy.

2 Pour the syrup into a bowl, add the lemon juice and leave to cool.

3 Meanwhile, blend the raspberries into a puree. Sieve the puree into the bowl of syrup, squeezing out as much juice as possible. Discard the seeds. Stir in the raspberry flavouring. Cover and chill for 30 minutes.

4 Pour the mixture into your ice cream maker. Churn and freeze according to your device's directions.

5 Serve and enjoy!

CHEFS NOTE

For more texture, don't bother sieving the puree and leave in the raspberry seeds.

RUSSIAN MELON SORBET

INGREDIENTS

- 600g/1lb5oz watermelon, peeled and diced
- 1 tbsp freshly squeezed lemon juice
- 2 tbsp vodka
- 250g/9oz caster sugar

METHOD

1 Blend the watermelon, lemon juice, vodka and sugar into a puree.

2 Pour into a bowl, cover and chill in the fridge for 20 minutes.

3 Pour into your ice cream maker. Churn and freeze, following your device's instructions.

4 Transfer the sorbet to a freezer container and freeze for 3 to 4 hours before serving.

CHEFS NOTE

This lovely, light recipe also works well with honeydew melon.

POMEGRANATE SORBET

INGREDIENTS

- 225g/80z caster sugar
- 250ml/8½floz water
- Large handful fresh mint leaves
- 450ml/15½floz pomegranate juice
- 200ml/7floz orange juice

METHOD

1 In a small saucepan, heat the sugar, water and mint leaves until it boils. Continue to boil, then boil for another 2 or 3 minutes, until the sugar has dissolved.

2 Remove from the heat and cool. Sieve into a bowl or jug, then stir in the pomegranate juice and orange juice. Cover and chill in the fridge for 30 minutes.

3 Pour the mixture into your ice cream maker. Churn and freeze following your machine's directions.

4 Serve and enjoy!

CHEFS NOTE

You could add a handful of chocolate chips towards the end of churning.

REDCURRANT SORBET

INGREDIENTS

- 450g/1lb redcurrants
- 300ml/10½floz water
- 2 tbsp elderflower cordial
- 140g/4½oz caster sugar

METHOD

1 In a pan, heat the redcurrants with a splash of water. Bring to the boil and simmer for a few minutes or until the berries burst.

2 Blend to make a purée. Stir in the elderflower cordial and set aside to cool.

3 In another pan, gently heat the caster sugar and water until the sugar dissolves. Turn up the heat and boil for 10 minutes.

4 Stir the redcurrant puree into the syrup and bring back to the boil. Lower the heat and simmer for a couple of minutes.

5 Remove from the heat, pour into a bowl to cool and chill in the fridge for 30 minutes, or until completely cold.

6 Pour into your ice cream maker. Churn and freeze according to your machine's instructions.

7 Serve immediately.

CHEFS NOTE

Looks and tastes beautiful garnished with a few whole redcurrants.

LEMON SORBET

INGREDIENTS

- 200g/7oz caster sugar
- 250ml/8½floz water
- 6-8 tbsp lemon juice
- Zest of 1 lemon
- 1 egg white, beaten

METHOD

1 Heat the sugar and water in a pan and stir until the sugar has dissolved.

2 Remove from the heat. Stir in the lemon juice & zest.

3 Leave to cool, then transfer to a bowl, cover and chill in the fridge for an hour.

4 Pour into your ice cream maker. Churn and freeze, following your device's directions.

5 Add the egg white and churn for just a little while longer, until the sorbet is firm.

6 Serve and enjoy!

CHEFS NOTE

You should vary the quantity of lemon juice to suit your own taste.

'CHEATS' BLACKCURRANT SORBET

INGREDIENTS

- 800g/1¾lb tinned blackcurrants in syrup
- 1 small egg white, beaten

METHOD

1 Blend the blackcurrants and syrup into a puree, then sieve into a bowl.

2 Cover and chill in the fridge for 20minutes.

3 Stir the egg white into the puree.

4 Pour into your ice cream maker. Churn and freeze according to your machine's instructions.

5 Serve immediately.

CHEFS NOTE

To make this even easier don't bother sieving the seeds out of the blackberry puree.

RHUBARB SORBET

INGREDIENTS

- 500g/1lb 2oz rhubarb, cut into chunks
- 250g/9oz caster sugar
- Juice and zest of 1 lemon
- 120ml/4floz water
- 1 tsp rhubarb flavouring

METHOD

1 In a pan, gently heat the rhubarb, sugar, lemon juice and water until the sugar dissolves and the rhubarb is soft. Remove from the heat and stir in the lemon zest and rhubarb flavour.

2 Allow to cool, then blend into a purée.

3 Chill in the fridge for 30 minutes.

4 Pour into your ice cream maker. Churn and freeze according to your device's instructions.

5 Serve and enjoy!

CHEFS NOTE

Fresh rhubarb is in season between late April and September in the UK.

MANGO & BLACK PEPPER SORBET

INGREDIENTS

- 4 ripe mangos, peeled, stoned and chopped into chunks
- 2 tbsp lime juice
- 60ml/2floz vodka,
- 350g/12oz caster sugar

METHOD

1 Blend the mango into a puree. Add all the other ingredients and blend again.

2 Sieve the puree into a bowl, cover and chill in the fridge for a couple of hours.

3 Pour the puree into your ice cream maker. Churn and freeze, following your device's instructions.

4 If the sorbet isn't firm enough to scoop, transfer to a container and freeze for 2-3 hours before serving.

CHEFS NOTE

No need to add the vodka if you want a booze free version.

LIME AND LYCHEE SORBET

INGREDIENTS

- 2 x 400g/14oz cans lychees in syrup
- 50g/2oz caster sugar
- 1 egg white, beaten
- 2 tbsp lime juice
- Zest of 1 lime

METHOD

1 Drain the syrup from the lychees into a pan. Heat gently with the sugar until the sugar has dissolved. Bring to the boil for 1 minute and remove from the heat.

2 Blend the drained lychees and pour these in the warm syrup along with the lime juice. Blend again until smooth.

3 Cool, cover and chill in the fridge for 30 minutes.

4 Fold in the egg white and the lime zest.

5 Pour into your ice cream maker. Churn and freeze according to your machine's instructions.

6 Serve immediately, or if the sorbet is not firm enough to scoop, transfer to a container and freeze for 2 hours first.

CHEFS NOTE

Delicious served with extra whole lychees.

PINEAPPLE SORBET

INGREDIENTS

- 120ml/4floz water
- 100g/3½oz caster sugar
- 450ml/15½floz orange juice
- 1 tbsp lemon juice
- 400g/14oz tinned pineapple
- Zest of 1 orange

METHOD

1 In a pan heat the water and sugar to a simmer until the sugar is dissolved to make a syrup. Remove from the heat.

2 Blend the pineapple with its juice into a puree. Pour it into a bowl and stir in the warm syrup and rest of the ingredients.

3 Cover and chill in the fridge for 30 minutes.

4 Pour into your ice cream maker. Churn and freeze according to your machine's instructions.

5 Serve immediately or transfer to the freezer for 2-3 hours for a firmer sorbet.

CHEFS NOTE

Fresh pineapple works too in this simple sorbet.

STRAWBERRY CHAMPAGNE SORBET

INGREDIENTS

- 225g/8oz caster sugar
- 300ml/10½floz champagne
- 350g/12oz strawberries, roughly chopped
- 1 tbsp lime juice

METHOD

1 In a pan, gently heat the sugar and the champagne until the sugar dissolves. Bring to the boil, add the lime juice, and gently simmer for 5 minutes. Remove the pan from the heat and leave to cool thoroughly.

2 Meanwhile, blend the strawberries to a smooth purée. When the syrup is cold, add it to the puree. Cover and chill for 20 minutes.

3 Pour the combined mixture into your ice-cream maker. Churn and freeze according to your device's instructions.

4 Enjoy!

CHEFS NOTE

Sieve the pureed strawberries if you want to get rid of the seeds.

RHUBARB AND STAR ANISE SORBET

INGREDIENTS

- 700g/1lb9oz rhubarb, chopped
- 150g/5oz caster sugar
- 75ml/2½floz water
- 2 star anise
- 1 tsp vanilla extract
- 1 tbsp lemon juice

METHOD

1 In pan, heat the rhubarb, sugar, water & star anise. Bring to the boil, stirring occasionally, then lower the heat and cook until the sugar has dissolved and the fruit is soft and starts to break down.

2 Remove from the heat. Take out the star anise and blend the rest into a purée. Sieve the mixture into a bowl, then stir in the lemon juice and vanilla extract.

3 Allow to cool, cover and chill in the fridge for 30 minutes.

4 Pour into your ice cream maker. Churn and freeze, following your device directions. Transfer the sorbet into a container and freeze for at least 3 hours before serving.

CHEFS NOTE

Star anise adds a fragrant spice infusion to this light sorbet.

PINK GRAPEFRUIT SORBET

INGREDIENTS

- 3 pink grapefruit
- 200g/7oz caster sugar
- 4 tbsp golden syrup
- 1lt/1½pt water

METHOD

1 Squeeze the juice from the grapefruit and set aside.

2 Heat the sugar, golden syrup and water in a pan. Bring to the boil, stirring to dissolve the sugar and cook for about 2 minutes until the liquid grows syrupy.

3 Pour the syrup into a bowl and leave to cool then chill in the fridge for 30 minutes.

4 When chilled stir the syrup into the grapefruit juice.

5 Pour the combined mixture into your ice cream maker. Churn and freeze following your device directions.

6 If the sorbet isn't firm enough to scoop, place it in a freezer container and freeze for 2-3 hours before serving.

CHEFS NOTE

Pink grapefruit is best for this simple sorbet.

PASSION FRUIT AND STRAWBERRY SORBET

INGREDIENTS

- 175g/6oz caster sugar
- 250ml/8½floz water
- 3 passion fruit
- 175g/6oz strawberries
- 1 tsp lemon juice

METHOD

1 In a pan heat the sugar and water together until the sugar has dissolved. Set aside to cool, then chill in the fridge until completely cold.

2 Scoop out the seeds of the passion fruit and finely chop the strawberries. Blend them with the lemon juice and syrup to make a puree. Sieve into a bowl to remove only the seeds from the puree.

3 Pour the puree into your ice cream machine. Churn and freeze according to your machine's instructions.

4 Serve and enjoy!

CHEFS NOTE

No need to sieve the puree if you prefer a coarser texture to your sorbet.

SIMPLE LIME AND COCONUT SORBET

INGREDIENTS

- 4 tbsp lime juice
- 400ml/14oz can coconut cream
- 175ml/6floz water

METHOD

1 Pour all the ingredients straight into your ice cream maker.

2 Churn and freeze, following your device's instructions.

3 Serve and enjoy!

CHEFS NOTE

Sorbet making doesn't get any simpler than this.

LIME AND BASIL SORBET

INGREDIENTS

- 200g/7oz caster sugar
- 250ml/8½floz water
- 23 tbsp lime juice
- 2 tbsp freshly chopped basil leaves

METHOD

1 Heat the sugar and water in a pan. Bring to the boil and cook for another minute or two until the liquid grows syrupy. Remove from the heat and cool.

2 Blend the syrup with the lime juice and basil to make a puree. Cover and chill in the fridge for 30 minutes.

3 Pour the chilled puree into your ice cream maker. Churn and freeze according to your device's instructions.

CHEFS NOTE

Basil and lime together make a delicious and refreshing dessert.

BANANA SORBET

INGREDIENTS

- 200g/7oz caster sugar
- 250ml/8½floz water
- 3 bananas, peeled & mashed

METHOD

1 Heat the sugar and water in a pan. Bring to the boil, cook for a minute or two more until the liquid grows syrupy, then remove from heat and cool. Cover and chill in the fridge for 30 minutes.

2 When the syrup is cold, stir in the bananas. Pour into your ice cream maker. Churn and freeze according to your machine's instructions.

3 Serve & eat!

CHEFS NOTE

If your bananas are very ripe you can reduce the amount of sugar in this sorbet.

FROZEN YOGURT

CHERRY FROZEN YOGURT

INGREDIENTS

- 200g/7oz caster sugar
- 225g/8oz cream cheese
- 1 tbsp lemon juice
- 600g/1lb5oz natural Greek yogurt
- 300g/11oz fresh cherries, pitted and chopped

METHOD

1 In a large bowl, stir the sugar into the cream cheese. Gradually add the lemon juice, and yogurt, stirring, until the mixture is smooth and creamy. Combine the cherries.

2 Cover and chill in the fridge for 20 minutes.

3 Pour the mixture into your ice cream maker. Churn and freeze following your device's directions.

4 Serve and enjoy immediately.

CHEFS NOTE

For an extra twist stir in some broken-up digestive biscuits.

BLACKBERRY FROZEN YOGURT

INGREDIENTS

- 200g/7oz blackberries
- 40g/1½oz caster sugar
- 300g/7oz natural Greek yogurt
- 50ml/2oz honey
- 100ml/3½floz milk

METHOD

1 Mix the blackberries and sugar in a large bowl. Leave for 30 minutes, then use the back of a fork to mash the berries.

2 In a separate bowl, combine the yogurt, honey and milk. Fold in the blackberry mixture, then cover and chill for 20 minutes.

3 Pour into your ice cream maker. Churn and freeze according to your device's instructions.

4 Serve at once, or firm up in the freezer for a couple of hours first.

CHEFS NOTE

Use ripe, seasonal blackberries to get the best flavour from this simple, delicious dessert.

RASPBERRY AND CHOC FROZEN YOGURT

INGREDIENTS

- 500g/1lb2oz natural Greek yogurt
- 250g/9oz raspberries
- ½ tsp vanilla extract
- 125g/4oz sugar
- 60g/2½oz dark chocolate, chopped

METHOD

1 Blend the yogurt, raspberries, vanilla and sugar into a puree. Sieve into a bowl to remove the raspberry seeds if you wish.

2 Cover and chill in the fridge for 20 minutes.

3 Pour into your ice cream maker to churn and freeze, following your machine directions. During the last few minutes of churning, scatter in the chocolate.

4 Eat and enjoy at once, or if you prefer a firmer texture, transfer it to a container and freeze for 2 hours.

CHEFS NOTE

Frozen raspberries work well for this dessert too.

SPICED PUMPKIN FROZEN YOGURT

INGREDIENTS

- 450g/1lb pumpkin, peeled, deseeded & chopped
- 375g/13oz natural Greek yogurt
- 8 tbsp maple syrup
- ½ tsp vanilla extract
- ½ tsp ground cinnamon
- ½ tsp ground nutmeg

METHOD

1 Cook the pumpkin in a pan of boiling water until soft. Drain, leave to cool & blend the pumpkin into a puree.

2 In a large bowl, mix the puree with all the other ingredients until smooth.

3 Cover the bowl and chill in the fridge for 30 minutes.

4 Pour the mixture into your ice cream maker. Churn and freeze following your device's directions.

5 Serve immediately or freeze in a container until needed.

CHEFS NOTE

Tinned rather than fresh pumpkin purée can also be used for this dessert.

MATCHA FROZEN YOGURT

INGREDIENTS

- 500g/1lb 2oz natural Greek yogurt
- 100g/3 ½ oz caster sugar
- 1 tbsp matcha green tea powder

METHOD

1 In a large bowl, whisk together the yogurt, sugar and matcha powder until the sugar is dissolved. Cover and chill in the fridge for 20 minutes.

2 Pour into your ice-cream machine to churn and freeze according to your device directions.

3 Serve immediately or transfer to a container and freeze for 3 hours to firm.

CHEFS NOTE

Matcha powder is a favourite with heath enthusiasts because of its high antioxidant properties.

STRAWBERRY FROZEN YOGURT

INGREDIENTS

- 450g/1lb fresh strawberries
- Juice of ½ lemon
- 400g/14oz natural Greek yogurt
- 150g/5oz caster sugar

METHOD

1 Blend the strawberries and lemon juice together to make a puree. Transfer to a bowl, cover and chill in the fridge for 20 minutes.

2 Stir the yogurt and sugar into the strawberry puree until smooth. Pour the combined mixture into your ice cream maker. Churn and freeze, following your device's instructions.

3 Serve and eat!

CHEFS NOTE

As well as their lovely sweet taste, strawberries are a great source of vitamins, minerals and anti-ageing properties.

GOOSEBERRY & ELDERFLOWER FRO-YO

INGREDIENTS

- 400g/14oz gooseberries
- 200g/7oz caster sugar
- 2 tbsp water
- 3 tbsp elderflower cordial
- 500ml/17oz natural Greek yogurt
- 150ml/5floz milk

METHOD

1 Gently heat the gooseberries, sugar and water in a pan. Bring to the boil and simmer for a few minutes until the berries soften.

2 Remove from the heat, allow to cool and blend into a puree.

3 Stir in the elderflower cordial. Transfer to a bowl, cover and chill for 30 minutes in the fridge.

4 In a separate bowl mix the yogurt and milk until smooth, then gently fold in the chilled puree.

5 Pour the combined mixture into your ice cream maker to churn and freeze according to your device instructions.

6 Enjoy!

CHEFS NOTE

This will keep well in the freezer for a number of weeks.

CHOCOLATE FROZEN YOGURT

INGREDIENTS

- 150g/5oz caster sugar
- 2 tsp cornflour
- 360ml/12½floz evaporated milk
- 100g/3½oz dark chocolate, chopped
- 200g/7oz natural yogurt
- 1 tsp vanilla extract

METHOD

1 In a pan, add the cornflour and sugar. Stir in the evaporated milk and chocolate chips and warm over medium heat, stirring constantly, until the chocolate is melted and the mixture is thickened.

2 Take off the heat and stir in the yogurt & vanilla. Cool, cover and chill in the fridge for 30 minutes.

3 Pour the mixture into your ice cream maker. Churn and freeze following your device directions.

4 Serve immediately and enjoy.

CHEFS NOTE

Use light evaporated milk and low fat yogurt if you want to make this a lighter dessert option.

ROASTED BANANA FRO-YO

INGREDIENTS

- 4 bananas
- 300g/11oz dark brown soft sugar
- 900g/2lb natural Greek yogurt
- 1 tsp vanilla extract

METHOD

1 Preheat the oven to 180C/360F.

2 Peel the bananas and halve them lengthways. Arrange them on a foil covered baking tray and cover them with the brown sugar. Bake for a few minutes or until the sugar melts and the banana is soft and roasted.

3 Tip it all into a large bowl. Cool, then cover and chill in the fridge for 30 minutes.

4 Then, stir in the yogurt and vanilla. Pour the mixture into your ice cream maker to churn and freeze, following your machine directions.

5 Serve immediately.

CHEFS NOTE

For more texture, drop some banana slices into the ice cream maker for the last few minutes of churning.

PEACH FROZEN YOGURT

INGREDIENTS

- 450g/1lb peaches, peeled and stoned
- 125g/3oz caster sugar
- 120ml/4floz natural yogurt
- 1 tbsp lemon juice

METHOD

1 Blend the peaches and sugar to make a smooth puree.

2 In a small bowl, combine the yogurt and lemon juice. Stir into the puree.

3 Cover and chill in the fridge for 20 minutes.

4 Pour into your ice cream maker. Churn and freeze according to your device instructions.

5 Serve and enjoy.

CHEFS NOTE

For the best taste use very ripe (or tinned) peaches.

MELON FROZEN YOGURT

INGREDIENTS

- 60ml/2floz water
- 50g/2oz sugar
- 1 small honeydew melon, peeled, deseeded & diced
- 250ml/8½floz vanilla yogurt
- 1 tbsp lime juice

METHOD

1 In a small pan, heat the water and sugar until boiling. Cook for a couple of minutes longer, stirring, to dissolve the sugar to make a syrup.

2 Transfer to a bowl and leave to cool.

3 Meanwhile, blend the melon into a puree. Pour it into a large bowl, then whisk in the cooled syrup, the yogurt and lime juice.

4 Cover and chill in the fridge for 30 minutes.

5 Pour the mixture into your ice cream maker. Churn and freeze, following your machine's instructions.

CHEFS NOTE

Try also with watermelon – just sieve to remove the seeds.

HAZELNUT FROZEN YOGURT

INGREDIENTS

- 60g/2½oz hazelnuts, toasted, chopped
- 1 tbsp brown sugar
- 2 tbsp hazelnut liqueur
- 600g/1lb5oz vanilla yogurt

METHOD

1 In a food processor, grind the nuts and brown sugar into a thick paste. Scrape into a bowl and stir in the liqueur and the yogurt.

2 Cover and chill in the fridge for 20 minutes.

3 Pour into your ice cream maker to churn and freeze according to your device's instructions.

4 Serve immediately.

CHEFS NOTE

Enjoy drizzled with chocolate syrup.

APRICOT FROZEN YOGURT

INGREDIENTS

- 8 fresh apricots, peeled & stoned
- 125g/4oz sugar
- 1 tsp lemon juice
- 1 tsp vanilla extract
- 600g/1lb5oz natural yogurt

METHOD

1 Blend the apricots, sugar and lemon juice into a puree. Stir in the vanilla extract.

2 Cover and chill in the fridge for 20 minutes.

3 Stir in the yogurt, pour the combined mixture into your ice cream maker. Churn and freeze according to your device instructions.

4 Serve immediately or store in the freezer until required.

CHEFS NOTE

If you can't get fresh, try with tinned or frozen apricots.

OTHER COOKNATION TITLES

If you enjoyed I Love My Ice Cream Maker *you may also like other titles in the* I♥MY *series.*

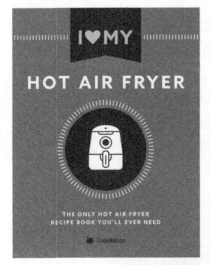

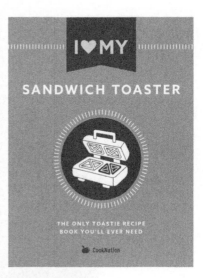

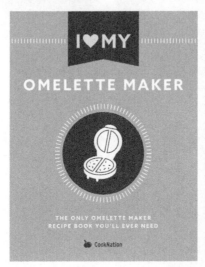

To browse the full catalogue visit
www.bellmackenzie.com

Printed in Great Britain
by Amazon

17681612R00054